Boot Camp for Christian Writers

2

I0446989

Writing-to-Publish: The Basic Foundations 2

"The Publishing Opportunities That Await You"

"How to Find Great Ideas to Write About"

Carolyn Tomlin

Writing-to-Publish: The Basic Foundations 2
by Carolyn Tomlin

Author Website/blog: www.carolyntomlin.com
Book design: Ellen C. Maze, The Author's Mentor www.theauthorsmentor.com
Cover Image and Interior Photos Credit: Carolyn Tomlin

ISBN-13: 978-1478309840
ISBN-10: 1478309849

All scripture was utilized from the New International Version (NIV) Bible translations unless otherwise noted in the text.

PRINTED IN THE UNITED STATES OF AMERICA

"Whatever you do, work at it with all your heart, as working for the Lord, not for men… It is the Lord Christ you are serving."

~ Colossians 3:12-17 & 3:23-24

Boot Camp for Christian Writers
Carolyn Tomlin

Writing-To-Publish: The Basic Foundations 2

"The Publishing Opportunities That Await You!"

Section I: In the first part of this book, I'll explain the type of articles in both the Christian and secular market that need your manuscript—work that will educate, encourage, entertain and inspire others through the written word! Learn editorial techniques for publishing, how to "break into" those markets, get your message across, and earn extra $$$.

"How to Find Great Ideas to Write About!"

Section II: Great ideas are all around you! Learn how to "see" with "writer's eyes," and "hear" with "writer's ears!" Discover how to glean ideas from your life experiences, your volunteer work, hobbies, career, family, and dozens of other aspects of living.

Section I and Section II contain written exercises to help the writer develop skills in these areas. They can be completed individually or in small-group settings with other writers. You'll find ways to extend learning, questions to consider, and discover interactive ideas with experienced writers.

A Personal Note to My Reader

This workbook is written especially for you—the **Boot Camp for Christian Writers®** boot campers. When you attend our all-day workshops, we are limited in time and cannot cover all the material you need. Corresponding to the workshop title, these books provide a deeper and more advanced study of the chosen topics. Designed to be used at home and when you have time to reflect, these books are a follow up to this seminar. After each section, space is provided for you to interact with the information. Use the additional pages to develop your own ideas by following the examples and format.

Writers can reach millions of readers annually through magazines. Writing can not only change the life of others—it changes your life, also! Our Boot Campers are people just like you. Perhaps you've thought of writing for years—but haven't started. Or, if you're like me, I thought no one would want to publish my work. Young people discover that writing can lead to interesting careers. Single parents earn extra money in this stay-at-home job. Seniors write their memoirs. And others turn an avocation into a vocation. You see, writing has no age limit. There's no retirement until "you" decide it's time to quit. An editor really doesn't care what you look like—or if you stay home and work in your PJs all day, or even if you comb your hair!

I've often said, "When the Lord knows it's best for me over there, in heaven instead of this earth, I hope someone finds me at my computer with my index finger on the "Send" key of my computer. And that my last manuscript "did" go through!

It is my prayer that writing will do for you—what it has done for me. And that you will develop a passion for writing and write articles and books that make a difference in the lives of others. Make God bless you as you write for Him.

~With all my best wishes, Carolyn Tomlin

Table of Contents

Section I:

The Publishing Opportunities That Await You

Chapter 1: Introduction –Developing a Writing Career –The Seasons of Life

For years I searched for something to fulfill this creative energy that was part of my life. During childhood my artistic side flowed by designing clothes for paper dolls, and then moved into making doll clothes. Soon, I was making all my clothes and even sewed for others. Like a woven tapestry, this thread of creativity was part of who I was; part of my every thought, part of my being.

As a child, books intrigued me. So did a new tablet. I recall the excitement when I sharpen a new pencil for the first time. Or, turned to the first page of a new spiral-back writing tablet. It was something about that fresh, clean paper that needed words to fill up the pages. Even the smell of a new tablet was exciting!

As I moved into the teen years, I entered the state fair where I won blue ribbons in sewing, flower arrangement and embroidery. By this time, I was making almost all of my clothes. In fact, my homemade dresses measured up to those in any store. Perhaps that's because my mother insisted the sewing be perfect. There was no room for "half-doing" anything. One of mother's favorite sayings was, "If it's worth doing, it's worth doing right!"

Into my life comes Matt Tomlin, a young, handsome ministerial student. Marrying at age 18, I made not only my wedding dress—a beautiful long-white satin gown with a long veil, but all my trousseau—known as "going-away" clothes. I never understood why the term was used for leaving on a 3-day honeymoon. Especially, when we returned, we rented a small apartment only five miles from my parents' home.

Marrying young has advantages – and sometimes disadvantages.

But looking back, I wouldn't change a thing. As a student-wife, I attended Union University with my husband. Matt served as pastor of a small country church. Driving over 2-hours each Sunday, taught us to trust in God in unseen ways. Somehow the tires on our old car usually got us there and back each week. Between the produce from my parents' garden, his parents pitching in and a church pounding each Christmas, we survived. You understand the word "pounding," don't you? That's where the congregation brings sacks or pounds of food. Once we received 15, five-pound bags of sugar. Plus, jars of canned green beans, tomatoes, jellies and pickles. How excited I was to fill my empty cabinets with all that wonderful food! Once again, imagination helped out when a meal consisted of a quart of home-canned tomatoes and spaghetti. God was taking care of us in ways we never thought to ask. Meat was a rare item.

Throughout my young adult years I tried numerous hobbies, projects and activities. Looking back, everything revolved around innovative ideas. Something new. Using my creative talent in a resourceful way. Being inspired by the natural world God created. Fascinated by designing clothes for myself and our daughter, I scanned Vogue Magazines and window-shopped at the best boutiques for women and children. Flower design, taking something worthless to others and turning it into a treasure for our home became a creative endeavor, and enjoying the challenge of using simple ingredients to make delicious meals. Creativity was at work—only taking different paths.

Finding Mentors

But with all these projects and activities, I was still searching. Then, one day I read that LifeWay offered a Summer Writing Conference where people could learn how to write and publish. My husband, Matt, and I attended. There we met Bob Hastings, one of the speakers who later became my mentor. Bob was the editor of the Illinois Baptist paper and was the author of many magazines articles and books. Readers will remember his *Tinyburg Tales*, a fictional place where all the women are strong, the men are good-looking, and all the children are above average.

Bob introduced me to editors and wrote letters recommending me for writing and speaking assignments. One editor was Charlie Warren, editor of Home Life Magazine. After submitting my first article to Charlie, he said, "If you will let me help you, I believe you will be one of the writers we call on regularly." Do you recall having an elementary teacher take a red pencil and make numerous corrections on your paper? Well, that's exactly what Charlie did. He cut it to pieces! It dripped red ink! I'm sure he spent several hours making changes and showing me how I could rewrite and edit. I'll never forget his kindness to help a new writer.

And yes, I did return home from the writing conference with two assignments. But I was the only one—I think. That's because during the course of the workshop, we were told not to bother editors and never to go directly to their second floor office. Well, as soon as the speaker spoke these words, I headed upstairs. There are times when rules are meant to be broken. This was the time!

Teaching as a Way of Helping Others

I often recall those dedicated teachers who patiently taught me the mechanics of writing. Spanning from first-grade all the way through graduate school, these professionals have made a difference in my life and the lives of others. Teaching is like a circle with no end. What we give to others—they pass it along. I owe them a debt of gratitude.

Coming from a family of teachers, my mother, aunt, female cousins and friends, I, too, chose a career in education. After teaching kindergarten students in public school to being Assistant Professor of Education at Union University, in Jackson, Tennessee, I completed thirty-three years of professional work as grant writer for the Jackson-Madison County School in Jackson, TN. Although I was teaching others to write, I still searched for that special spark that wasn't part of my life. That is until I wrote and sold my first article, *Living with Teenagers*, a Christian magazine published by LifeWay. "How to Communicate with Your Teen" was accepted and published in 1989. Now at last, I was a published author and life has never been the same.

Creativity takes numerous forms. Like the seasons, we, too, change. Perhaps I wasn't ready to write-to-publish until I was 48-years-old. But I can't imagine my life without putting words on paper—now a computer—and using my original ideas to communicate with readers.

Recently a woman asked me how I wrote so many articles. My reply, "You only have to know the 26 letters of the alphabet and numbers 1 – 10 and you can write anything." Well, maybe there's a little more to writing than that, but you understand the idea.

About this time, I met Denise George at a writer's conference. Isn't it strange how God gives us opportunities and it's up us to take advantage of these events. Already seasoned writers, Denise and I took a break from the session and ended up on an outside porch. An editor had suggested I might like to meet this woman—whose name was Denise George from Birmingham. I looked at her—she looked at me—and we introduced ourselves. And from that time on, we've been best friends. God is good! He had a plan that would take us on a journey that neither of us could imagine!

Boot Camp for Christian Writers

Denise and I continued our writing ministry. Mine, mostly magazine articles and Denise, books. People we met asked us questions, such as: How did you start writing? What makes a difference in receiving a contract instead of a rejection letter? How can I network with other writers and editors? How can I write to inspire, educate, inform and entertain others and what I write be to glorify God? Endless questions. Unknown answers that needed asked.

After asking God how we could help others know this passion that we possess, we decided to start a writing ministry for women, called "For Women Who Love to Write." After several weekend retreats, men starting requesting that they attend, also. To accommodate them, we started our Boot Camp for Christian Writers, an all-day event where we teach writing-to-publish.

By the year 2012, we've taught over 1,000 people to write-to-publish. Beeson Divinity School on the campus of Samford University in Birmingham, AL has generously provided support and space for our workshops. We are under the umbrella of the Lay Academy of Theology and promoted in Beeson mailouts. In west Tennessee, Union University in Jackson, TN is working with us to offer Boot Camps for people in this area. Through various media, such as newspapers, radio and television interviews, we are contacting people. Churches sponsor those unable to attend. People telephone about future seminars. Interest runs high.

As we reach more people who have a dream of writing-to-publish, we pray that we can be an instrument in the hands of God. That we will give godly advice, encourage our Boot Campers and be supportive as they network with others.

Chapter 2: Why Do We Write?

There are many reasons why people write—and various reasons why people never put pen-to-paper and publish. Of course, today, it's turning on the computer, emailing electronically instead of going to the post office and sending a hardcopy of the manuscript and buying postage.

Do you ever wonder how great writers of the past, wrote in long-hand, without the use of a spell-checker—yet, still turned out manuscripts that have stood the test of time? Think about Henry David Thoreau, sitting in a small cabin on the banks of Walden Pond and writing great manuscripts—by hand. The apostle Paul in prison—writing in a dark, damp cell, on anything he could find to transcribe thoughts. Imagine the early typewriters used by William Faulkner and the Braille machine used by Helen Keller, a blind woman, from Alabama, who changed the world for those with a handicap.

The writing life is much different today than in times past. However, the imaginative and inspired thoughts will always set writers apart from others. Are you someone who calls yourself a "writer?" Do you see things differently than ordinary people? If so, thank God for that innate streak of creativity that allows you to see things with different eyes and different ears.

Look at the following reasons we feel led to write:

1. To Honor God

There are many reasons why people write. As Christians, we should write to honor God. Philippians 4:8-9 says, "Finally, brothers, whatever is true, whatever is noble, whatever is right, whatever is pure, whatever is lovely, whatever is admirable—if anything is excellent or praise-worthy—think about such things. Whatever you have learned or received or heard from me, or seen in me—put it into practice. And the God of peace will be with you." What a promise! We know that God has kept his promise in the past—he will continue to do this if we honor Him with our lives and our writing.

Name 3 ways your writing can honor God?

1._____

2._____

3._____

2. To Reach People

Magazines reach Millions.

Words are a powerful tool to change the lives of readers. If you want to reach millions of readers—write for the magazine market. Are you interested in the number of people who may read your article? Here's how to check:

- Check the Writer's Market for the circulation number for each magazine in which you publish articles. If this is unavailable, call the toll-free number and ask the circulation of the publication.

- Editors believe each magazine is read by at least 3 people. However, this number is probably higher. Think of all the places you've seen popular magazines. Such as health clinics, beauty shops, libraries, schools and others.

- Add the weekly publications (such as newspapers) or monthly magazines for which you write. Are you surprised? Magazine writers have an opportunity to reach millions of readers each month. And the numbers reach to millions and millions annually. If you have a message to relate to readers, the magazine market will put your words in the hands of masses of people.

Writing for the magazine market reaches more people than most speakers or book writers reach in a lifetime.

Check the circulation number for 3 magazines you would like to submit articles. (Look in the Writer's Market.) If you wrote for this magazine once a year, how many people read your article? What if you wrote every month? If you wrote for 5 magazines every month, what is the number?

Name of Magazine   Circulation Number

1._____   _____

2. _____   _____

3. _____   _____

Magazines Reach People

Magazines Reach People	
• American Profile	10,000,000
• Mature Living	350,000
• SBC Bulletin	10,000
• Growing Magazine	25,000
• The City News	15,000
• Baptist & Reflector	40,000
• WMU, Mission Friends	10,000
• Children's Ministry	65,000
• Pentecostal Evangel	265,000
	--------------
1 Month total	10,880,000
10,880,000 X 3 =	32,640,000

Make a list of (5) Christian and (5) secular magazines that you would be interested in submitting articles.

Christian Magazines

     1._____

     2._____

     3._____

     4._____

     5._____

Secular Magazines

     1._____

     2._____

     3._____

     4._____

     5._____

3. To Help Others

Writers help readers discover a passion for living. Albert Einstein, a genius who contributed much to our lives, said, "A life lived for others is the only one worth living."

Think of the way an article can help others. Articles provide tips for being a better parent, to budget your financial resources; to grow spiritually; to improve your marriage; and to find ways to volunteer in your community. And there are thousands of others.

List 3 ways you can help the reading audience find a passion for living through magazine articles or books.

1._____

_____

2._____

_____

3._____

_____

4. To Develop Your God Given Talents

The Scripture encourages us to use the skills and talents God provides us. In Matthew 25:14-30, Jesus gives us The Parable of the Talents. Here again, Jesus illustrated through stories how He wants us to live our lives. You recall the story of how a master entrusted his servants with his money. To one he gave five talents, another two, and to another one. The first, put his money to good use and made another 5 talents, which gave him 10. The same for the servant with two talents—who now had 4 talents. But the servant with one talent hid his talent in the ground. When the master returned, he praised both men who now had increased their talents. He was so pleased; he gave them other responsibilities and put them in charge of many things. But for the servant who buried his talent, the master was very disappointed. In fact, he took his talent away and gave it to the one with ten talents. Verse 29 says, "For everyone who has will be given more, and he will have an abundance. Whoever does not have, even what he has, will be taken from him."

What lesson is Jesus teaching us? That if we use the talents he gives, he will bless our work and we will be given even more responsibilities. And if we fail to develop our talents or skills, they are lost. It's true of those who write and ask God to bless their lives.

Writers touch millions through magazine writing. You can be a writer who reaches the masses!

Think about this:

---

1. How does the Parable of the Talents apply to you?

_____

_____

2. How can you make better use of the skills and talents God has provided for you?

_____

_____

Chapter 3: Opportunities Are Everywhere

The world in which we live offers a plethora of ideas for writing. It's a common saying, "Children learn best through their senses." If this is the basic, most innate way of learning, why not use the senses in your writing to describe your thoughts?

- ➢ Seeing
- ➢ Hearing
- ➢ Smelling
- ➢ Tasting
- ➢ Touching

Traveling and Photography Provide Opportunities for Writing

There are two types of readers that pick up travel articles. One, those who will visit the site; and two, armchair travelers. In writing travel articles, you want to encourage the reader to visit the site. Or if an armchair traveler – one who is unable to travel but still wants to experience the culture, environment and senses of the location – you entertain and educate through words.

Travel writers realize photos are often the key in receiving an assignment. Make plenty of photos. You may not return or have a second chance to capture that image. With digital photography, you can make hundreds of shots at no cost. Before digital cameras, I spent a fortune on film and developing. Often, I had only one or two that were suitable for publishing.

What subjects will you look for in making photographs? This depends on your area of writing. Also, do you have assignments from a magazine before you leave on the trip? If so, focus your camera on the type article you will submit.

Photographs Can Tell a Story

Look for photographs of people, places, and things when searching for article ideas.

> **People**—Look for ordinary people, workers and local artists. Search for faces that tell a story, people wearing clothing native to the country and families spending time together.
>
> If you plan to photograph a person showing their face, ask their permission. In the U.S. have a permission form available. (In foreign countries, I do not use this—unless an official or a recognizable person.) Offer to pay a small amount. For one-dollar, I received permission to make a picture of a Chinese sampan boatman dressed in a hand-made, water-repellent hat and coat from tree bark; a rickshaw driver; the farmer who discovered the Terra-Cotta Warriors on his land; a Russian woman selling wild flowers; a Holocaust survivor along the Volga River, a fisherman repairing his lobster traps in Nova Scotia and many others. As I write the assigned article, these photos rekindle my memory and help tell the story I'm submitting.

In China, boatmen maneuver the sampans through the tributaries off the Yangtze River. He has crafted a hat and coat made from tree bark that sheds water.

➢ **Places** – What makes you want to go there? How can a photograph encourage you to know more?

Be honest—do not lead readers to believe it's a utopia if you wouldn't want to go there—again. However, I look for the good. Most people find what they're looking for. If you expect to have a good trip—you will. If not—you'll be disappointed.

Cathedral of St. Basil the Blessed (built in 1555-1561) while Ivan the Terrible was Czar of Russia. This structure is composed of eight churches and is one of the most photographed buildings in Red Square, located in Moscow, Russia.

➢ **Things** – After viewing your photographs, what crafts, plants, animals or objects would encourage an editor to send a contract?

Alaskan totem poles tell a story to honor a proud heritage. Crafted in stylistic animal and human figures, they are painted in symbolic colors to illustrate legends.

Chapter 4: What Are Your Reasons for Writing?

Ask any number of writers this question and you will have as many different answers. People want to become a writer for various reasons. Articles may be divided into these four categories: To educate, to encourage, to entertain and to inspire.

- You have something to share.
- You have survived, walked-through, or experienced this topic or situation.
- You want to explore this topic.
- You write about things you know—or things you have an interest in learning.
- You use writing as an avocation that later becomes a vocation.

Writing to Educate

Words are powerful. Did you know those 26 letters of the alphabet can change the thoughts and minds of people? Education takes many forms—such as:

- Moving from one to two morning church services.
- Adding a daycare program to your church.
- Encouraging more people to go on volunteer missions.
- To show people the need for change.
- Encourage a teen to prepare for college or job training.
- To maintain a healthy body through exercise, nutrition, rest and relaxation.

Tai Chi is a form of exercise that people of all ages can participate in. These senior adults meet every morning in Beijing, China.

The following travel article on China (first published by *Mature Living* Magazine, May 2007) is an example of educating the reader on ancient China as well as today's modern cities. The title clues the reader as to the focus of the article.

China: Yesterday and Today

By Carolyn Tomlin

The China of yesterday is one of the oldest civilizations known to man. In this land once ruled by Emperors, architectural remains tell the story of how people lived and worked. Located on the eastern part of Asia, the land covers 3.7 million square miles and has over 1.3 million people or 1/5 of the world's population. In the cities, family apartments and office buildings compete for land space and high-rise structures often reach 50 floors. With more people owning cars, city streets are congested and filled with bicycles, taxis and tour buses. Yet, in the older areas of the cities and especially on the small rural farms, life continues as it has for generations.

Beijing, The Capital City

We begin our visit in Beijing, one of the six ancient capital cities of China. Tiananmen Square or "Gate of Heavenly Peace" is located in the heart of Beijing and is one of the world's largest public squares.

Occupying an area of 720,000 square meters, the Forbidden City is a place where commoners were forbidden entry for over 500 years. Also known as the Palace Museum, this municipality was the imperial palace of Ming and Qing dynasties. With construction beginning in 1406, the site boasts a history of 600 years. It's here that 24 emperors ruled China for nearly five centuries.

The 9,000 halls and rooms of the Forbidden City contain marble railings and steps with red walls and yellow tiles. Tradition says that only the emperor could use bright colors and private houses must be gray or earth tone. With a moat surrounding the outside walls, the Forbidden City became a strongly fortified castle. Bronze lions guard the entrance to some of the buildings, signifying power, dignity and luxury. Over 300 two-ton, gold-plated bronze and iron vats were originally used to collect rain water and placed on the exterior walls to extinguish fire.

Traveling by rickshaw is a common site through the "Hutongs" or the old town of Beijing. Strong young men ride bicycles on which a covered bench is attached. Due to the narrow streets in the Hutongs, rickshaws are the best means of transportation.

The Great Wall—One of the Wonders of Human Civilization

A short bus ride from Beijing is The Great Wall, one of the magnificent construction projects of ancient China. Astronauts report one of the defining moments in space is viewing the Great Wall that winds along like a 4,000 mile long dragon. During the 7th and 8th centuries B.C. and continuing for over 2000 years, over 20 dukes, princes and feudal dynasties contributed to its construction. Built to keep marauding Barbarians from attacking the country, the wall also kept the people from leaving the area. Lookout towers provided guards easy access to the surrounding countryside.

As visitors climb the slab stone steps and uneven walkways, one is reminded of the treacherous mountain tops. It has been said for every foot of the Wall, a worker lost his life. Listen, and you can almost hear the winds carrying the sound of distant hoofs that was built to allow five horses to gallop abreast or ten soldiers to march shoulder to shoulder.

The Three Gorges Project

The largest water conservancy project ever undertaken by man is the Three Gorges Dam. Built in Sandouping, the site is located in the middle of the Xiling Gorge, and the longest and most dangerous of the three gorges on the Yangtze River. The Qutang Gorge is known as the most magnificent gorge and the Wu Gorge is the most beautiful. When completed in 2009, the estimated cost will be 230 billion Chinese Yuan (28 billion U.S. dollars). Its purpose: flood control, electricity, navigation and irrigation. Over 570,000 acres of farmland, villages in 19 counties and cities will be flooded, causing 1.5 million people to be relocated to areas above the flood plain. High-rise apartment buildings dot the skyline as a new way of life for many residents along the Yangtze River.

Yangtze River Cruise

Flying from Beijing to Yichang, our tour group boards the Victoria Anna--a cruise ship that will transport us along the Yangtze River. Due to silt washing from the hillside farms, the river appears a muddy brown in color. Small family farms dot the rugged mountain slopes where generations of people continue to grow small gardens of vegetables and fruit trees.

Some stretches of the Yangtze remain untouched as farmers plow the soil on steep hillsides. Then suddenly, a city of millions of people comes into view. Skyscrapers like giant Lego Blocks® dot the landscape. Statistics show that 1/12 of the world's population live in cities along this river and the valley is home to 1/3 of China's population. Chongqing has over 33 million; Fengdu 760,000.

At Wushan, we boarded sampans to travel the smaller tributaries of the Yangtze. Sampans are lighter boats able to seat about 20 people and guided by local men. Once we left the Yangtze, the Daning River turns a beautiful blue-green shade. Up close, we saw wild monkeys, beautiful birds and flowers growing in the rocky bluffs. Life has changed little in these inner canyons over the centuries. People of the Ba Kingdom once lived here over two thousand years ago and entombed their nobles in coffins suspended high in cliff crevices. Look close and you see the "Hanging Coffins" on the steep cliffs.

The cruise ends at Chongqing, a picturesque mountain city that clings to rugged mountain ridges. Known for its unusual weather, the city averages 68.3 days of fog per year. And in summer, Chongqing is known as one of the "three furnaces along the Yangtze.' Temperature can reach as high as 116 degrees Fahrenheit with the humidity between 90 and 95 percent.

While in Chongqing, stroll through the Panda Zoo and photographer the famous black and white bears chomping on their daily diet of bamboo. Pandas often eat 14 hours per day and spend the rest of the time sleeping.

Terra-Cotta Army

In 1974 a farmer was digging a well and discovered pottery fragments and ancient bronze weapons. The local government was alerted and news of the treasure aroused national attention. Asleep under the ground for over 2200 years, stands the Terra-cotta Army of the Qin Dynasty. These warriors, weapons and other objects of the era are regarded as 'the Eighth Wonder of the World." The size, large number and exquisite artwork are considered miracles of art in terms of their excellent workmanship and showcase the talents of ancient China.

However, what is seen today is the Terra-cotta Army that has been reconstructed piece by piece by archaeologists. After the Emperor Qin's death in 210 B.C. the farmer's revolt took place in retaliation for the area's wealth being buried with the ruler. Local peasants smashed, burned and destroyed most of the figures.

Today, you can visit the Terra-cotta Museum located on the east side of the Mausoleum of the first emperor in Chinese history. A walkway allows visitors to look down into the three excavated pits. One sees faces showing individual features of the warriors, horses, and bronze chariots—all vital to the afterlife. Archaeologists continue to unearth other remains of the Qin Dynasty. Nearby is the Emperor's Mausoleum which remains unopened.

By visiting China, you'll appreciate the culture and heritage of an ancient land as well as explore modern day cities. Shopping, dining and entertainment are available and accessible by taxi or bus. Tour groups provide excellent service and English has become a second language. You'll find the Chinese people friendly and helpful as they welcome visitors to their country.

Carolyn Tomlin writes travel articles for numerous magazines. She is the co-teacher of Boot Camp for Christian Writers. (End of article.)

China's great wall covers over 4,000 miles and runs from west to east. The structure was built to keep marauding Barbarians from entering China.

Writing to Entertain

Laughter is good for the heart and mind. Proverbs 17:22 reminds us that "A cheerful heart is good medicine, but a crushed spirit dries up the bones." Research says that we need 12 good laughs a day to stay healthy. Can you make an editor laugh? Can you use humor without using racial or cultural derogatory language? Many people can tell a funny story—yet few, can write one. If so, humorists are in demand. Magazines use humor for the following areas:

- Fillers and jokes
- Cartoons
- Personal experience, where you laugh at yourself—not others.
- Children's stories where the main character discovers something funny and solves the problem himself.

Rocky learns good table manners. (Why is this funny? It's unexpected in training a dog.)

The following filler, published by *Country Place* Magazine, comes from a personal experience of being a parent.

Trick or Treating Was "Ruff, Ruff"
By Carolyn Tomlin

When our children were of trick-or-treating age, they never failed to dress up and go door to door seeking candy treats. But when they sang the doorbell, the homeowners were just as likely to hear "Ruff! Ruff!" as they were to hear our children's cry of "trick or treat!" That's because our Irish setter, Big Red, thought he was just another one of the kids when it came to Halloween.

Big Red followed the children everywhere when they left our yard, and Halloween was no exception. He even got in the spirit by being dressed in a costume, much to his delight. His attire was usually my son's old swim trunks, a necktie, floppy hat, and sunglasses.

As the children visited neighbors in our rural area, Big Red carried his own plastic pumpkin for collecting his bounty. When my son rang the doorbell at each home, Big Red always pushed in front of the group and sat patiently holding the pumpkin bucket handle in his mouth, ready for a treat.

Tootsie Rolls were by far his favorite, but chocolate chip cookies came in a close second.

While the children enjoyed their Halloween night out, my husband I didn't have to worry. We knew they were safe with Big Red escorting them from house to house. (End of Article)

Writing to Encourage

Life is not always easy and day-to-day living may be filled with problems along with happiness. There are many times we need encouragement. Writers can make a difference in over-coming those times when a crisis comes. There are many times in life we need encouragement. Could you be the writer who made a difference?

- Loss of a job
- Adult returning to college
- Sickness or death of friend or family member
- Natural disasters
- Financial crisis
- Depression
- Accidents

The following article "Preachers Can Communicate Through the Written Word" was published by *Preaching* Magazine (April 2006). I wrote this article as a way to encourage those in Christian education to write –to-publish. With forced termination of some pastors, writing offers options to a second career. This article shows the basic techniques for being published.

Preachers Can Communicate Through the Written Word

"Their voice has gone out into all the earth, their words to the ends of the world." - Romans 10:18, NIV

People who preach the gospel have many ways to use their Spiritual gifts. For some, this means pastoring a church. For others, it means serving on the mission field. Or, a person may dedicate their life to teaching children, youth or adults in Sunday school. And a few seek the Lord's leadership by writing for the Christian market.

As a writer for religious publications, preachers have the opportunity to touch the lives of multitudes every week, every month. For example, an inspirational message on the back of a church bulletin reaches over 300,000 weekly. And many Christian magazines send a message to 50,000 or more each month.

As a writer, realize the awesome responsibility you've been given to share the love of Jesus with thousands. How can you use your gifts? What writing tips make a difference in being published? What type of magazine articles can be directed toward the Christian market? (End of Article)

Writing to Inspire

Writing for the Christian market offers many opportunities to write articles that inspire. Look at some of the following ways:

- To share a Spiritual truth
- To inspire others to action
- To instruct teachers to develop interesting curriculum that reach students
- To entertain children through Bible activities that teach

Use photos to provide inspiration for writing. The first photo was made on Union University's campus in Jackson, TN after the Feb. 2010 tornado. When congregations realized the destruction, many groups volunteered their services. Faculty, staff and the community gave room and board to students. Only a few days of classes were missed. By the fall of 2010, new buildings and dormitories were ready. Photos inspire people to action. Use them to help you start an article.

Or, offer a photo/article package when proposing an article to an editor. Look at the beautiful butterfly below. Check a guidebook if you're unsure of the species.

List 3 ideas that a butterfly would lend to an inspirational article.

1._____
2._____
3._____

Suggestions for Being Published

What makes a difference in your article being accepted – or ending up in the trash can? Depending on the writer you ask, you will receive a variety of answers. Experienced writers agree: these tips will help you submit an article for publication.

- Study several copies of a magazine before submitting a query letter or manuscript. You ask: *How can this help?* By showing a profile of the people who read this magazine. Look at the age of the people. Are they young families, or senior adults? Advertisements provide a clue to the economic level of the readers. For example, do travel articles   cover exotic, expensive locations – or does the text suggest ways to enjoy traveling on a budget?

Another reason for reading back copies: Does the magazine publish articles offensive to the Christian lifestyle? Would you, as a writer, want your name in this publication?

- When quoting Scripture include complete, accurate references and the particular version used. Check writer guidelines for the preferred version.

- Always honor deadlines. Editors must meet their schedules. Building a reputation as a writer who beats deadlines gives you an advantage. In fact, email or use postal mail, early. Avoid last minute work. If you had to rush, your work likely will indicate it.

- Expect to edit and rewrite. Many writers make a first draft on magazine articles by putting down thoughts quickly. Then, they go back and edit and rewrite. By allowing the manuscript to "get cold" and reading again in a couple of days, you see the words in a new light.

- When you query an editor, mention that photos are available. Learn to use a digital camera and email pictures along with articles. Smaller magazines lack the resources to send a photographer to the location.

- Serious writers understand the importance of using technology. Today, with Internet connection, scanners, email, and computers a writer can work and never have to leave the comforts of home. Although these tools make work easier, they are not necessary to producing copy for the Christian market. However, all magazines insist on typed copy—not handwritten. If you do not type, locate a person in your church and pay them to type your work. Then you may email, or send a CD to the publication.

- Collect writing ideas from everyday life. Listen to conversations as you wait in a grocery line. While listening to a speaker, take notes. As you read inspirational books, keep a note pad nearby.

- Use your five senses in writing. Children, especially, learn best this way. How can you describe a beautiful sunset created by God? Using words, show the reader how the bark on a tree feels to the bare hands. Test your olfactory senses by pulling in the fragrance of a beautiful rose. Think of your senses as a gift from God -- one that makes the world a better place.

- Block off time for assignments of different lengths. For example, if you are assigned a long Sunday school curriculum unit, schedule a time each day and commit yourself to write.

- As you become more experienced, you'll find shortcuts to save time. Keep a journal of these tips that work for you.

- Make a daily writing schedule. Jot down deadlines on your calendar. Do you need to email an editor about an assignment? Where can you find data on the number of new churches established each year?

- When writing a query letter, send published clips of your work. For example, you want to write a travel article for a Christian senior magazine. Sent clips of a published travel article focusing on seniors. If you have not sold articles, include in the query letter that you have traveled on senior trips, mentioning sites that are friendly to older adults who might need special assistance. Always include a self-addressed stamped envelope (SASE).

- Use sidebars for material that supplements the regular article, yet doesn't seem to fit into the body of the manuscript. This breaks up the article and provides interest to the reader.

Focusing on Magazine Articles

Writers share their faith by inspiring others to action, by instructing teachers to develop interesting curriculum that reach the audience and by entertaining children through Bible activities that teach. The following article types lend themselves to the Christian market:

> **Inspirational** – If you can use temporal objects to relay a spiritual truth, the inspirational market may be for you. Think of ways to encourage a new church member, to equip young parents who have moved their membership to your congregation, or to uplift a person's spirits.

> **Humor** – Many people can tell a funny story, yet few understand the mechanics of writing one. If you can make an editor laugh, you'll find many opportunities for this style of writing. Can you use an anecdote to make a point?

> **How -To** – Two basic kinds of how-to articles are *project* and *problem-solving*. Both are straightforward and require a step-by-step process. In the project article, the reader learns how to make a Bible school craft, the advantages of doing it and reassures the simplicity of the project. The problem solving speaks of a concern (such as how to help your church grow),

advice from a recognized leader or an anecdote that illustrates a point.

> **Travel** – Did you know that travel and tourism are major industries? Therefore, travel articles continue to increase in popularity. Think of locations where church groups might visit. Is there a site available for youth groups? Include activities of interest to the readers, information on lodging, restaurants, and wholesome entertainment.

  Realize that not everyone who reads your article will actually travel to this destination. Some remain "arm-chair" travelers. Therefore, make your information interesting material that educates as well as entertains.

> **Interview/Profile** – Closer to a biography than other articles, the profile uses comments from others to give total personality coverage.

> **Questions & Answer** – In ten to twenty questions, the writer provides questions and the subject of the article gives the answer. Or, it might consist of several authorities in the field. For example, ask a series of questions on how small churches provide activities to reach young people and teens.

Both novice and veterans writers benefit from attending Christian writing conferences. Check the *Cross & Quill: The Christian Writers Newsletter* for an update at www.cwfi-online.org. For an annual listing on writing for the Christian Market, use Sally E. Stuart's Christian Writer's Market Guide, Harold Shaw Publishers, Wheaton, Illinois.

Writing for the Christian market is a ministry. God calls preachers to communicate His word to the world through both speaking and writing. Pray that God will guide you to use the highest quality of biblical and professional standards as you reach multitudes for Christ.

Chapter 5: How to Break Into the Magazine Markets

After publishing over 3,600 magazine articles in the last 20 years, I stopped counting. Breaking into new markets is always a challenge. These approaches work for me. Can they make a difference in you receiving more contracts than rejection letters?

- Networking. If I had to name the best way to break into new magazine markets, networking would be Number 1.
  Writers must work at meeting editors, agents and publishers and keep these contacts up-to-date. Get to know the secretary or the person who handles the phone. Someone who knows someone, who knows someone can recommend you for an assignment.
- Write for multiple magazines within the same company. Find companies that publish more than one magazine. Develop a positive working relationship with this editor. Ask them to recommend you to another editor with one of their magazines. Often editors are in cubbies or across the hall. If you're proven to meet deadlines and be easy to work with, chances are you will find other magazines within the same company eager to assign you articles. After an editor has recommended you, write a letter of introduction and a query. Know the magazine and audience for which you want to write.
- "Show" that you are a responsible person. When I receive assignments, I write the due date on my desk calendar at least 2 weeks before the editor's deadline. Emergencies happen. Personal responsibilities take control of our lives. Don't let a deadline slip up or be late. After publishing over 3,600 magazines articles, I can say, "I've never been late,

once." This is one reason writers who "Do what they say, they will do," get repeat business.

- Check guidelines.

What is Your Link or Connection?

Think about your talent, employment experience and volunteer work. This determines the type of magazines and books where you will have a greater success rate. Are you interested in the following areas?

- Music
- Education
- Missions
- Agriculture
- Travel
- Ministry

List additional areas not mentioned.

1._____
2._____
3._____

Use Your Hobbies as a Way to Publish

What do you enjoy—just for fun? Woodwork, sewing, leather design, or crafting jewelry? I have to admit—I'm a gardener through and through. In fact, my gardening interests go back generations. As most of my family lived into their nineties, and a grandmother died 6 months short of one-hundred, they knew something about living the good life until the Lord called them home. Looking back, they all loved to be outside working in the sunshine, digging the good earth and finding time to smell the flowers. Did they discover the "fountain of youth" through gardening?

Because of my interest in planting, growing and learning about plants, I've published hundreds of articles in this area. I'm not certified in agriculture or horticulture—I just enjoy gardening. But I have excellent contacts that have degrees in this field that I call when needed. It's important in writing to provide other resources than your own. The following is an example of writing a gardening article that was published in several Christian magazines.

Gardening Through the Winter
By Carolyn Tomlin

"As long as the earth endures, seedtime and harvest, cold and heat, summer and winter, day and night will never cease" (Genesis 8:22). After the time of Noah and the Flood, God promised that the earth would follow a pattern --a sequence that man could depend upon. And with this order each season carries responsibilities, especially for those who garden.

After frost and freeze signals the end of the growing period, gardeners still find many winter duties in preparation for the following spring. Perhaps seniors have downsized to a smaller lot or one with less outdoor work. Have you forgotten some important chores that will make your garden and yard easier to maintain next season? Look at the following checklist.

- Concrete birdbaths and large pots may crack in freezing weather. Drain and cover with heavy-duty plastic bags.
- Provide alternative sources of water for wildlife. Use an electric warmer and replace fresh water often.
- Remove old mulch from under bushes and shrubbery where insects can breed. Replace with pine straw to protect against cold weather.

- Store patio umbrella to guard against high winds. Secure outdoor furniture.
- Undergrowth on fence rows provides habitat for birds and small wildlife. Think of their needs and wait until warmer weather to remove.
- Remove piles of leaves from the grass or mulch with a mower. After a rain, heavy leaves can suffocate your yard. Use to improve your compost collection.
- Sketch a draft of plants for the coming season to plant near your entrance.
- Start a garden journal for the coming year. Make note of the weather, planting time, date when flowers bloom and new varieties to try for the coming months.
- Request seed and plant catalogs by calling their toll free numbers or web addresses.
- Purchase or make garden artwork and plaques to bring joy to your space.

Even in winter, a gardener's work is never done. Seniors who enjoy this healthy hobby earn food and thoughts to nourish the soul.

_____

Carolyn R. Tomlin gardens in Jackson, TN. (End of Article.)

Are You a Collector?

Some people collect antique carnival glassware—I do. Others collect first-edition books—my husband does. And I have a friend that collects dogs—lots and lots of dogs! Like a river that changes course as it meanders through a valley, we have stages in life when we pursue different interests. In recent years, mine has been Southern Folk Art. Now I'm not talking about the expensive items found in art galleries or craft fairs across the country. I'm talking about those one-of-a-kind roadside finds put out for the garbage truck.

Most recently, I rescued a 125-year-old white iron headboard, a wheelbarrow (rusty, of course with a hole in the bottom) —perfect for a planter with a drain, and an antique screen door—which I propped under a huge pecan tree nestled between two blue Adirondack chairs. Tie these treasures together with colorful glass bottles suspended on bushes and painted tomato cages turned upside down and you have a backyard that you don't want to leave. Throw in multiple bird feeders and birdbaths and you enjoy a symphony complete with carolers. Does it get any better?

I'm saying this: Think about what you enjoy. Write it up. Sell the article for first rights. After that, sell it as a reprint many times. Not only will you earn enough for more bird food, flower bulbs, cans of spray paint (for the rusty wheelbarrow painted bright yellow), but you'll encourage others to develop that eye for turning trash-into-treasure.

The following article was published in several newspapers.

Using Folk Art in the Garden
Subtitle: Bottles, Bicycles and Tail Pipes: Treasures in the Garden

Seniors are known for their creative ability to "make do, use it up, or do without." Perhaps it's that work ethic philosophy stemming from the Depression Years or World War II. Whatever the reason, American Folk Art is alive and well in today's gardens.

If straight line rows, boxwoods clipped to perfect mounds or formal English designs leave you cold, perhaps using folk art in the outdoors is for you. Or if you had rather share a glass or lemonade under a shade tree with a friend, instead of pruning, keeping the edges neat, and controlling all weeds, think about adding a nostalgic feeling to your patch of green.

Remember: There are no rules to using folk art in the garden. One person's trash is another's treasure.

Starting Your Collection

Think creative when starting your collection. Whimsical and imaginary accent pieces can divide the yard into rooms or interest areas.

- **Glass Bottle Tree**

  Begin by collecting a variety of shapes and colors of small glass bottles. Wash to remove labels or inside residue. Invert bottles on branches of a small tree. Or, fill a large outdoor planter with soil or rocks, insert bare limbs and turn bottles or small clear vases upside down on the branches. Smaller ones work best as they do not pull down the limbs. Secure around the neck with florist wire. Place a spotlight behind the tree to illuminate after dark. Enjoy your original stain glass creation as you share with family and friends.

- **Bicycle Folk Art**

  Before those 10-speed bicycles came into vogue, people rode simple bikes designed for either males or females. Check your garage, basement or yard sales for these relics of the past. Painted in bright colors, they make a conversation piece when located in strategic places of the garden. Could morning glories climb the spokes? Could a wicker basket be attached to the handlebars for trailing petunias or ivy?

- **Iron Headboards**

  Did your grandmother's home contain at least one iron bed? Those ornate headboards are making a comeback as garden art. As you need only the head of the bed, look for mismatched pieces in second-hand stores. Vines, such as Clematis or Chinese Jasmine need little encouragement to twist and twine around the posts and curved frame.

- **Farm and Automobile Relics**
  Who would ever believe those rusted pieces of tailpipe could become the body of an imaginary insect? Sanded and painted – the only limit is your imagination. And where are these items found? Search repair shops for farm machinery or country garages. Don't overlook country back roads for car parts that have fallen by the wayside.

Using folk art in the garden brings out the child in seniors. Ask your friends to look for unusual objects. Then, get together and plan a day of fun and creativity. It's a no-season, whimsical approach to using unlikely objects for garden decoration.

_____

Carolyn Ross Tomlin, Jackson, TN, searches for far-fetched items to use in folk art gardening. (End of article.)

Turn colored glass bottles upside down on a bush or tree. Morning sunlight and a spotlight at night bring a smile to those who view your art. Using photographs can make a difference in you receiving a contact.

Chapter 6: Publishing Tips That Sell Articles

Think back in your life to when you really wanted something. You worked for it, exchanged something of equal value or did without. Breaking into the magazine market can be difficult, but certainly attainable. Realize that you often start by writing for "free," meaning that you are paid in contributor copies. After I had written for about 20 years and had more than 3,600 magazine articles published, a magazine editor that I queried said: We don't pay for articles. But we will send you three copies of the magazine – at no cost! These will be a conversation piece on your coffee table!" I thought—if you only knew! If every editor had "paid" in contributor copies, the huge stack would have pushed through the roof of the house.

But there are times when writing for "free" is the way to land an assignment later. If you have a message to share, and one that will make a difference in the life of another—wouldn't it be worth the honorarium? Writing is not about you—it's not about the money!

What makes a difference in you being published or ending up in the slush pile? Look at the following ideas as to breaking into a new magazine market.

- Networking – Probably the most important factor in getting published.
- Multiple magazines with the same company.
- "Show" that you are a responsible person.
- Honor deadline, check guidelines. What is the "lead" time between accepting an article and publication?
- Be courteous to editors.
- When receiving a contract, ask for the editor's input or suggestions.
- Read back copies. Check archives for on-line magazines.

- Use complete, accurate references for Scripture. Check guidelines for the preferred version.
- Expect to edit and rewrite.
- Write a query for your article—especially with a new market or editor.
- Writer guidelines tell the preferred method of contacting an editor and sending a manuscript. Will they allow phone calls? Email? Or, snail mail? Follow these rules.
- Mention photos when you query an editor. Photos can often sell your idea. For example, most magazines cannot send a photographer to film your travel location.
- Understand and stay informed on current technology. Always submit a computer-typed article. Save a copy.
- Collect ideas from everyday life.
- Use the five senses as you write.
- Block off time for assignments. Do a task-analysis of long assignments, such as curriculum or unit writing. Plan the number of hours per day, or per week, until the deadline.
- Realize the deadline is when the article should be on the editor's desk or emailed. If a hardcopy is required and the deadline is only a couple of days away—send by over-night carrier. However, don't allow yourself to be caught in this situation. This practice tells the editor you did a rushed-job.
- Keep deadlines on a calendar. In fact, write the due date about 2 weeks early. Give yourself time for unexpected events.
- Keep a list of shortcuts that work for you. You are an "original." Use your creative talents of things that work for you—not necessarily for others.
- Make a daily writing schedule. Before bedtime, I make a brief "to-do" list of my next day's writing activities. Often it's only one word—such as an email to an editor, a query to a specific magazine, completing an article and finding the perfect digital

photo. If you know what you need to accomplish each day, you'll stay focused and complete the task.

- Submit published clips of your work with your query—especially for a first-time market. Hopefully, you'll have clips that focus on a similar topic you're querying. If not, send another published clip. This way, the editor assesses your writing style.

- Study the magazine format. Does the magazine use bullets, sidebars, and a section "for additional information?" When writing your article, keep the magazine nearby and follow the same format as used. Don't try to re-invent the wheel. Your role is not to change the magazine's style.

- Use a pen name if needed. Once I wrote an entire magazine using seven different pen names. Following the editor's suggestion, I use a combination of my maiden, my mother's maiden name, my paternal grandmother's maiden name, my own and the initials for my first and middle name. Why did I do this? The editor said that if a reader noticed my name with all these articles, they would complain. (Sure they would!) Perhaps this would be the reader who had tried unsuccessfully to be published and seeing my names throughout, would be upset. (Wouldn't you?)

Chapter 7: Differences Between the Secular and Christian Market

Christian writers contribute to both the secular and Christian market. As a writer, who is a Christian, I would never write anything that would go against the laws of God. I ask myself: would God be pleased with my thoughts and words? Could this article inspire, educate, inform, and encourage the reader to take action, to have a better life, to improve their marriage, to handle their finances in a way that glorifies God or to be a better parent?

Usually, an article for a Christian publication includes Scripture. However, Bible verses may be found in articles for the secular market, also. The Amy Awards are given to a writer who has an article in a secular magazine that includes Scripture.

The qualities of a Christian writer include compassion. Philippians 2:4 reads, "Each of you should look not only to your own interest, but also to the interest of others." When we've gone through the valleys of life—and they will come—we gain strength and wisdom when we come out on the other side. We know God is near. He has walked through the rough times with us and we are not alone. What have we learned? How can we use these insights to help others? This is the joy of being a writer—to feel another's sorrow, to experience another's pain, to walk in their footprints.

As a Christian, and trying to do the will of God, this verse in Matthew 7: 7-8 helps me live day-to-day. "Ask and it will be given to you; seek and you will find; knock and the door will be opened to you. For everyone who asks receives; he who seeks finds; and to him who knocks, the door will be opened."

Think About This:
If you have a desire to write, what should you pray for?
List those areas.

_____

_____

_____

How is God Working in Your Life?
List those areas.

_____

_____

_____

Notes from Section 1:

Section II:

Finding
Great
Writing Ideas

Chapter 8: Using Your Senses to Find Writing Ideas

"In the same way, let your light shine before men, that they may see your good deeds, and praise your Father in heaven."
Matthew 5:16

Do you believe great ideas are all around you? When you train your senses to be aware of the world around you—ideas fill your mind.

Each of our five-senses is a gift from God. Through sight, hearing, smelling, tasting and touching, we gain insight in the world God designed. These gifts make our lives better and allow us to enjoy the beauty of His creation.

Researchers believe that young children learn best through their senses. If this is correct, could writers use these terms to help describe their work?

➢ See with Writer's Eyes

Using the sense of sight, use each word in a sentence.
For example: (Apple) Some of the red apples appeared shiny; others dull.

1. (Banana)_____

_____

2. (Parrot)_____

_____

3. (House)_____

_____

➤ Listen with Writer's Ears

Using the sense of hearing, use each word in a sentence.

1. (Firecracker) _____

_____

2. (Marching band) _____

_____

3. (Washing machine) _____

_____

➤ Taste with writer's taste buds

Using the sense of taste, use each word in a sentence.

1. (Cinnamon) _____

_____

2. (Lemon) _____

_____

3. (Ice cream) _____

_____

➤ Smell with writer's olfactory senses.

Using the sense of smell, use each word in a sentence.

1. (Smoke)_____

_____

2. (Roses)_____

_____

3. (Sardines) _____

_____

➤ Touch with writer's hands.

Using the sense of touch, write each word in a sentence.

1. (Corduroy fabric)_____

_____

2. (Kitten's fur)_____

_____

3. (Moss on a tree trunk)_____

_____

Consider These Sources for Ideas

- Life experiences
- Volunteer work
- Hobbies
- Two-career family
- Your childhood
- Family history
- Nature
- Pets

Let's look at the topic of "Hobbies." Or, perhaps you place this under gardening. I do. One of my hobbies is taking something old and useless to others and creating a thing of beauty. In other words—trash to treasure. In my backyard, I've turned a mid-town acre into a secret garden filled with Southern Folk Art. Of course, my husband calls if Tennessee Trash. The eyes of the beholder, determines what it's called. Often while driving, I'll spot a rare find, hit the brakes and make a quick turn-around. Parking on the roadside, I'll release the trunk button, hurry to the pile waiting to be picked up by the clean-up crew, and load my treasure into the trunk without getting run over by traffic. Just recently, I spotted a rusted wheel-barrow that needed some TLC (tender, loving, care). Fortunately, the rusted bottom already had a hole for drainage. Using a wire brush, I scraped the bottom and sides clean. Next, came a primer coat to keep the rust from bleeding though. Then, I painted the entire wheelbarrow bright yellow with Williamsburg blue handles. Filled with pine needles, I placed seasonal pots of plants inside. For summer, the container overflows with green and purple sweet potato vines and several varieties of coleus. For fall planting, mums will replace the summer annuals.

When thinking of using this as a magazine article (and this is the one reason I enjoy this) I make digitals from beginning to the end of the project.

Why am I including this? Because, you can use your creativity to enjoy a craft or hobby, write about it, get paid, encourage others to use your ideas and have fun while working.

A rusted wheelbarrow is turned into an attractive container for holding a variety of plants. Rotate plants for seasonal beauty.

Another idea is to use discard items to help others and publish as an article. *Mature Living* Magazine (Feb. 2012) published an article on using plastic grocery bags to make sleeping mats for the homeless. Editor Rene Holt reported that over 500 people or groups requested more information on this article. This means thousands of people became involved in a mission project and thousands of homeless people received a gift from a church that says "Jesus Loves You." The article follows.

Sleeping Mats for the Homeless

"...Whatever you did for one of the least of these
brothers of mine, you did for me."
Matthew 25:40

Instead of discarding plastic bags, senior adult groups in churches are turning them into sleeping mats for homeless people. Similar to the traditional rag rugs made by your grandmother, plastic bags are cut into loops, which are crocheted into serviceable pads. This project provides a washable sleeping mat that keeps moisture away from the body, creates warmth on cool nights and offers a soft surface.

During winter months, churches and other organizations, provide over-night sleeping accommodations, meals and Bible study. Room at the Inn is one such program. However in warm weather, a program such as this may cease. By providing the homeless with a sleeping mat, you're showing others that God cares for them.

Materials
Plastic bags (clean, grocery story variety, between 500-700 per mat)
Scissors
8 mm or size "P" crochet hook
Cardboard guide
Bible thought card. Print "God Loves You."

Directions
- Place bag in a lengthwise position.
- Fold in half, then fold in half again.
- Cut off bottom seam and top handles. Discard or recycle.

- Place bags on the guide so measurement is the same. Cut regular supermarket bags into 2.5-inch loops. For thicker bags, cut into 2-inch loops and thinner bags—cut into 3-inch loops.
- Cut loops and connect in the following way: Pick up two rings (or loop). Place one end through the other. Place the end of the second strip through itself. Pull both ends until tight.
- Repeat steps and roll length into a large ball.
- Write a Bible thought and connect it to the mat.

Crochet Directions
- Using a size "P" crochet hook, make a chain 36-inches long.
- Make loops loose with space between each loop.
- Crochet one extra loop the end of the chain for a turning point.
- Return to the third loop to make row two.
- Continue until the mat is 6-feet long.
- Crochet from front to back to avoid puckering. (A finished mat measured 3-feet by 6-feet.)
- For a tie, crochet two rows of single loops to make an 80-inch string.
- Connect the tie to the middle top. This allows the mat to be rolled up for transporting.

Plastic bags turned into sleeping mats have become a year-round project that is being used as a mission emphasis in churches. It's a small way of expressing the love of Christ to others. Not only the homeless, but places where natural disasters such as earthquakes, floods, and tornadoes have occurred are welcoming these gifts. It's an easy, no-cost project for both men and women and which requires no previous experience.

Pray for the person who receives this gift from your church or organization.

_____

Carolyn Tomlin writes for numerous Christian publications. She is the co-founder and teacher of "Boot Camp for Christian Writers." Email: carolyn.tomlin@yahoo.com. (End of article.)

Plastic bags are cut and tied into strips to make sleeping mats for the homeless. This is mission project can involve various ages in your congregation.

Ideas for Gratitude

President John F. Kennedy said, "Ask not what your country can do for you. Ask what you can do for your country."

When you're searching for ideas, begin by writing down ideas of gratitude. In six words or less, share what you're grateful for.

For example:

- God, family, friends, America, chocolate, coffee
- Green lights, indoor plumbing, spell checker
- Bumping into random acts of kindness
- Comfortable shoes, cotton sheets, fluffy towels.

Write three of your own:

1. _____
2. _____
3. _____

When Your Well Runs Dry

I believe the more you write, the more ideas you'll find. For some writers, this is easy. For others—it's work. Perhaps it's your attitude toward the topic or just the stress from daily living that keeps us from generating ideas. These approaches have helped me when I can't think of anything to write.

- Write a "thank-you" letter in a local newspaper.
- Keep a gratitude journal three times a week.
- Practice an act of kindness daily.

- When you first awake each morning, ask God to show you someone to encourage each day.

Perhaps your well runs dry when you continue to procrastinate too often—over too long a period. As a writer, I work best and ideas seem to flow when I write daily. If I go several days without composing an article, well frankly—I have trouble getting started. Words from Mother Teresa stay in my thoughts.

> *"Yesterday is gone: Tomorrow has not yet come. We have only today. Let us begin."* ~ Mother Teresa

Procrastination is an enemy of writers. We put off today what can be done tomorrow. Maybe you've fallen into the trap of "There is always tomorrow." If you've thought about writing, prayed about writing, even purchased books on writing and attended writing conferences—the time is now.

List three things that keep you from writing. How can you make changes in your life so that you can realize this dream of writing-to-publish?

1._____
2._____
3._____

Overcoming Writer's Block

Some people experience writer's block often—for others, it's not a problem. My suggestions:

- Start typing or writing on a pad—write anything. Just write.

- Open the dictionary. Close your eyes. Let your finger fall on a word.

- Write the word down.

- Continue until you feel an inspiration to write.

- Write daily. Journal, a note to a friend or correspond with someone.

- Read from favorite authors.

An idea just came to you. Jot it down here:

_____

_____

_____

_____

_____

_____

_____

Chapter 9: Articles Titles That Sell

Article titles catch an editor's attention and secure a contract. Use a play on words of a familiar quote, book, song or movie. Check table of contents for titles in magazines. Are they humorous? Does it give basic information? Does the title provide clues as to material found in the article? Put yourself in the reader's place. Does the title interest you? By understanding the article titles in the magazine, you'll improve your chances of receiving an assignment.

Look at these titles and how they relate to the reader, as well as the magazine:

> *Deacon Magazine* – "Looking for Love in All the Right Places." The readers are wives of pastors. The magazine is for deacons and those in Christian ministry.

> *Mature Living* Magazine (October 1996) – "Putting Your Garden to Bed." This article gives advice to amateur gardeners on preparing your garden for the cold, winter months. The target audience focuses on senior adults.

> *Cats* Magazine (December 1991) – "When Bad Things Happen to Good Cats." The magazine is for cat owners. The article provides guidelines for understanding why cats may misbehave or become bored. Offering suggestions for keeping cats safe and entertained when the owners are away, the topic is approached in a humorous way.

➢ *Brownsville States Graphic* –"How to Build a Cat House." House cats are descended from those of the wild. Those early ancestors hunted at night and slept in trees to stay safe from predators. Today's indoor cats need places to climb and enjoy fresh air in a safe environment. The solution? Build a screen room where your cat can have the best of both worlds.

Finding Ideas for a Story

It happens to all of us. One day our cup is filled with ideas. The next, we can't think of anything to write. Look at the following situation.

Situation:
You can't think of anything to write about. Or, you think, *my life is so ordinary. I haven't done anything interesting—especially that anyone would want to read.*

Solution:
- Open your eyes.
- Look around you.
- Take a walk.
- Listen to snippets of conversation. Standing in line at the grocery store gives some very interesting dialogue for your next novel or article.
- Do chores that require no thought, such as: pull weeds in the garden, take a warm shower, wash dishes in a sink filled with warm water, iron clothes. While doing these chores, pray for your family and friends. Pray for the person whose dishes you wash or clothes you iron.

Chapter 10: Going to the Source for Ideas

I advise writers to write about things they know, but to also write about things they want to know. What if an editor contacts you for an interview article on a farmer? Or, a teacher? Or, a pastor? If you are not a farmer, teacher, or pastor—what can you do? You go to the source! Find someone who is respected in their area and write your interview. If this person works for someone else, include this person as a source. Who are others who might add to your article? Asking for quotes and bits of conversation, others supply information for you. Always check the reference for accuracy.

Consider these questions to get you started. Think about open-ended questions that encourage more than a "yes" or "no" answer.

1. ## What's it Like to Be a Teacher?
   - How did you make a difference in the life of one student?
   - What techniques do you use for classroom discipline?
   - If fights have irrupted, what caused them in your school?
   - What are some characteristics of a school bully?
   - Follow the bully into the next grade. Paint a word picture of "before" and "after."
   - Explain how you solved a parent problem?

   List factors that affect teachers today that would be helpful to someone choosing education as a career._____
   _____
   _____

2. What's it Like to Be a Farmer?

- How do you deal with summer drought, heavy spring rain and weather that affect your crops?
- How did you control the herd of deer that feasted on your soybeans?
- How does the cost of insurance cut into your profits?
- What alternative crops may prove beneficial when planting next year?

List concerns a farmer faces that would be helpful to others who grow the food we eat._____

_____

_____

3. What's it Like to Be a Pastor?

- You feel God calling you to serve another church? How do you tell your family?
- Comment on health problems that can be caused by stress.
- Another church has offered an invitation to be their pastor. Your children are active in high school programs.
- Your spouse is employed in high-paying career. A move means he/she loses her job.
- Your elderly parents live nearby. How will a move affect them?
- Church members are taking sides in a political debate. How will you handle this situation so that your congregation is not affected?

List issues facing a pastor today that would be helpful to others in this ministry?

_____

_____

_____

Chapter 11: Using Personal Experiences for Story Ideas

God made us different and we possess unique personalities. Although we may share physical characteristics within the same family, no two people on earth are exactly the same. When you interview people expect to receive different viewpoints. This makes for interesting reading.

1. List family stories you could write, such as: vacations, reunions, extended families, sibling relationships.

2. What is special about your pet? Does he like one family member over another? Does she beg for certain foods? Does your pet recognize your moods?

3. Start with "Remember when..." Don't write chronologically. A pattern will usually emerge for random stories. Such as:
    *   The time Mrs. Clifton left out the lemon in the lemon pie.
    *   The Christmas that Sears Roebuck didn't connect with Santa. (Santa arrived on Dec. 27.)
    *   The time a huge grasshopper jumped down my dress in a church revival. (The church windows were open, no air-conditioner and the temperature was near 100 degrees.)

➢ Write From Your Point of View and that of Others

- Interview different family members as to their memory of an event.
- Accept the fact that different ages recall unique images when retelling family history or stories.
- Interview older family members about an event in history. What do they recall?

➢ Use Dialogue as People Tell Their Own Story
When writing someone's story, allow the dialogue to carry the story along.

- Dialogue makes stories more interesting.
- Use a colloquial saying that people will identify with as coming from that individual. My grandmother Milner often said, "Well, that's the way they do it up home." "Or, that's what they 'wear' up home." Of course, "up home" was a very, small, west Kentucky community. My mother's familiar saying was, "Well, you can't have everything." These words of wisdom have helped me accept whatever happens in life. And my mother-in-law, Ethel Tomlin's favorite saying was "Well...maybe, so." You didn't argue with her as the matter was settled. There was no changing her mind. So by adding dialogue, you give the reader a glimpse into the personality of the character in the story.

Write some favorite sayings from your family or friends. Use these as dialogue when describing characters in your writing.

_____

_____

_____

➢ Use Family Pets in Your Writing

If you're like most families, you've had pets that were part of your family. We had Mama Dog and Little Puppy. These were strays and we didn't think they would hang around for long—therefore, they were never named. However, they stayed and came when called.

As a child, we had Mama Cat who had four kittens, which we named Petunia, Buttercup, Pansy, and Daisy. All names of flowers and all girl names. However, all four were males and went through life with female names. Imagine being the neighborhood Tom Cat with names like these!

Weave family pets and stories into your writing. Is your dog afraid of thunder? Do you have a cat that eats corn-on-the-cob? A horse that loves sugar cubes? Does your dog appear to smile when you enter the room? Rocky, our Pomeranian actually hides his eyes when he doesn't want to obey. He thinks if he can't see us, we can't see him.

One look at Rocky's face tells you he is guilty!

➢ Use Ideas from "Then" and "Now"

Use your creativity when writing "then" and "now" articles. Have fun and add a smile to the reader's face.

1. What if early pioneers traveling west had a cell phone? Write a humorous story about staying in touch with family back home.

2. What if Paul Revere had used email instead of riding a horse to warn the colonists that the British were coming? Who would be listed on his "contact" list? Write a story showing the simple way Revere could have contacted neighbors in his area and gone to bed early.

3. What if Moses had downloaded the 10 Commandments he received from the Lord on Mount Sinai? Write a story showing the problems that might develop, such as someone hacking into his computer, his computer crashes just as No. 10 goes through, or lighting strikes and causes an electrical shortage.

Take a historical account and write a "then" and "now" situation. Have fun and allow your creativity to soar!

_____
_____
_____
_____
_____
_____
_____
_____
_____
_____
_____

➢ Find Stories Ideas in Everyday Life
Used in writing newspapers articles, answering these questions will help as you write other types of manuscripts. The writing is like a puzzle with several parts. When you've answered these questions, your article is basically, written.

1. Why?
2. When?
3. Where?
4. What?
5. How?

Think like a reporter.
Read a newspaper article.
Circle these five questions.
How did the writer transition from one to the other?

Chapter 12: Articles Ideas Promote Your Book

Marketing takes many forms. You may work with a large publisher but it's still up to the author to promote the book. This is where writing articles is vital to the success of your text. As the co-author with Denise George of *The Secret Holocaust Diaries: The Untold Story of Nonna Bannister,* we've written dozens of articles and spoken over 150 times on the book. With the circulation of magazines in the thousands, a writer has an opportunity to speak to millions of readers each year. I've explained how editors believe each magazine is read by at least three people. Add the monthly readers; now add the annual. The numbers are astounding!

Study the magazine market in the Writer's Market and the Christian Writer's Market. Become familiar with several magazines that focus on your genre. Study back copies—usually available online. How can you write an article that fits the format of the magazine while promoting your book? Yes, it takes work. But the rewards are seeing your text becoming an awarding winning book and the sales increase.

The following article was published by the *Women's Journal,* (Oct.-Nov. 2009) a regional west Tennessee publication. Although several local newspapers and journals had published an article on the book, I took a different slant and wrote about life in the prison camps during the Holocaust and how some women survived by learning to trust and make friends with others.

Carolyn Tomlin   First Rights
5 Greenway Drive
Jackson, TN 38305   Word Count – 691 in text

The Secret Holocaust Diaries: The Untold Story of Nonna Bannister
Subtitle: The Role of Women in the Prison Camps
By Carolyn Tomlin

The Secret Holocaust Diaries: The Untold Story of Nonna Banister, published by Tyndale House (April 2009) is a true story of Nonna Lisowskaja, a young Russia girl. Nonna was the only one of her 35-member family known to survive the oppressive nature of Russian Communism and the viciously evil heart of Nazi Germany. Written from the diaries of Nonna Bannister, co-authors Carolyn Tomlin and Denise George put the text into book form.

The book is an account of childhood, the war years, the prison camps and after the war when she arrives on American soil. Written from diaries and tiny slips of paper, she wrote in six languages so the Nazis could not translate the diary if discovered. How the book came to be is another important part. Because Nonna didn't want to relive the horrors of the past, she waited 46 years to share the story with her husband, Henry.

One important feature of the book is the role of women in the prison camps. Reviewers have said it's one of the best documents of the life of women behind the barbed-wire fences and how they formed social groups that helped them endure the difficult conditions. Crossing social and cultural barriers, the friendships that existed between women formed relationships that often saved their life.

By 1942 Nonna and her mother, Anna, are the only family left after everyone else is missing or has been killed. Cold, hunger and fear are daily enemies. They hear of factory work in Germany—work that will provide a salary, food and shelter. Anna buys a train ticket to Germany only to realize they are prisoners, just like the Jews on a cattle car on an adjacent track.

For days the women are packed, like sardines in a can, as they travel east. SS soldiers and dogs guard each car. Finally arriving in Kassel, Germany, they are assigned to work in a carton factory. Before daylight each morning, they rise, step in line during roll call, and march for two miles, often in extreme cold. For their one daily meal, they receive a small ration of greasy water called "cabbage soup" and a cup of weak tea. In the barracks, Nonna and Anna slept on a hard board with only a thin blanket for cover. Winter temperatures often drop to -35 degree below zero.

Sharing meager food allowances helped the women endure prison conditions. Anna, being an accomplished artist and violinist often painted large murals for the Nazi officers. Christmas 1942, the Kommandant rewards her with a bag of cookies from his wife. Nonna says the women always shared any extra food so that everyone had a little something. The officer found a pine branch for a Christmas tree—even colored construction paper and glue. All the women sang Christmas carols in their native language. Nonna tells of how beautiful the voices blended—each in their own tongue—while singing the familiar Christian carols.

Another way the women survived the endless hours was to create card games Anna drew from scraps of paper. Friendships developed. Socialization took root.

No one knew what the next day would bring. Would someone be called out and never be heard from again? Would a new-found friend die from a simple infection or lack of medicine? The women tried to take care of each other and developed strong friendships that brought comfort. Yet, it took time to learn who could be trusted—and who could not.

Nonna's story continues and after the war she comes to America. The Secret Holocaust Diaries is a story of forgiveness and how faith in God carried her through the darkest hours of the Holocaust. Nonna's is only one story—

but it's a story that represents thousands, if not millions, of other Jewish and eastern European families.

Carolyn Tomlin and Denise George are the co-authors of *The Secret Holocaust Diaries.* They lead writing-to-publish seminars and present programs on the book. (End of article.)

"The Lord bless you and keep you. The Lord make his face to shine upon you, and be gracious to you. The Lord lift up his countenance upon you and give you peace."
~ Numbers 6:24-26

Notes from Section 2:

Also by Carolyn Tomlin

The following books, in hardcopy, paperback, and as ebooks, can be ordered and/or downloaded through amazon.com as well as other outlets.

What I Wish I'd Known Sooner: Parents
By Carolyn Tomlin
Do you ever wish the things about being a parent hadn't taken you so long to learn? This book is part of a series and focuses on the joys of being a parent. Bits of wisdom the author learned from raising two children are interwoven with prayers. You'll laugh, and rejoice in this role of "Parenthood." Section two, The Home and School Connection, offers guidance and self-help for parents as they deal with school-related issues. You'll find answers to Bus Safety, Making Friends, Peer Pressure, How to Talk with the Teacher, and other topics.

What I Wish I'd Known Sooner: Teachers
By Carolyn Tomlin
Part of a series, this book is written for educators. Included are bits of wisdom, prayers for teachers and students. Chapters are divided into areas affecting teachers, such as First Day of School, Open House, Bus Duty, and others. This series has been used in speaking to teacher groups, given as a gift and as a quick read for those who are able to laugh instead of cry when facing situations that arise in everyday life. Prayers give the reader strength and courage.

More Alike than Different (story and coloring book)
By Carolyn Tomlin, illustrated by Ellen C. Maze
This is a story of Matthew, a young boy, who makes friends with children in his community from different cultures and ethnic groups. He soon learns that God made and loves all children and that we are all "more alike than different." Black and white line drawings provide a kinesthetic form of learning as children color the simple pictures.

The Secret Holocaust Diaries: The Untold Story of Nonna Bannister by Nonna Bannister, Carolyn Tomlin and Denise George

Nonna Bannister almost carried a secret to her Tennessee grave. As the only known family survivor of the Holocaust, she came to America after the World War II, married Henry Bannister and did not tell him about being a Holocaust survivor for over forty years. Hidden under her dress, her grandmother tied a little ticking pillow filled with family photos. In this pillow, Nonna kept her secret. It's a true story of a little Russian girl who survived because of faith in God, love of family and the ability to forgive her enemies. This award-winning book was Published by _Tyndale House Publishers._

The following books are out-of-print but may be available on www.half.com, www.amazon.com **or other outlets.**

Teachers as Published Writers

A practical guide to writing and publishing for teachers. Readers will learn how to know the magazine market, understand the reader's needs and sell ideas developed in the classroom. Other teachers will benefit from your ideas across the curriculum. Published by _Judy Wood Publishing Company._

From the Cat's Point of View

Written for cat lovers, this book gives a glimpse inside the mind of our furry friends. Can cats read your mind? Do they relate to your emotions? Read looking at life through the eyes of a cat to discover more about yourself—as well as that of your feline.
Published by _Judy Wood Publishing Company._

More Alike than Different, (A children's story book)

Focusing on accepting multicultural differences, Matthew, a young boy meets the people in his neighborhood. Written as an easy-reader and as a listen-to-me book, children will soon be repeating the phrases uses over and over again. Published by *WMU Publishers.*

Mental Pause

Taking a humorous approach at menopause, the author describes emotions and behaviors related to this time in a woman's life. Published by *Judy Wood Publishing Company.*

True Tales or Tall Tales: You Decide with Denise George and Carolyn Tomlin

Some stories are just too strange to be true—or are they? Based on stories from the news and the writer's creativity, you will not know if this is a true story or a tall tale. Turn to the back of the book to find the answer. Written for upper elementary and middle school students. Published by *Judy Wood Publishing Company.*

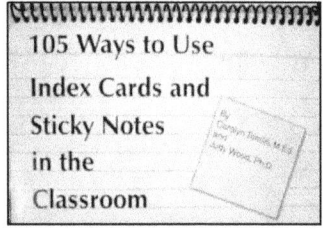

105 Ways to Use Index Cards and Sticky Notes in the Classroom, Judy Wood and Carolyn Tomlin

This book offers suggestions for using index cards and sticky notes in all areas of the curriculum—from reading, math, science, social studies and others. Published by *Judy Wood Publishing Company.*

A Parent's Guide to Summer Survival

School's out! The long-awaited summer vacation has finally arrived. For most kids, it's approximately 10 weeks (or 70 days, or 1,680 hours) each summer. For students, nothing could be better. For parents, what will you do with the kids all day? Instead of fussing, being bored, or having a "panic attack" try some of the great ideas in this book. Published by *Judy Wood Publishing Company.*

365 Email Messages for Students and Teachers (with Veronica Coulston) Make using the Internet and Email fun for students! Teachers find questions from the curriculum based on history, fine arts, sports, literature, social studies, science and other topics. Each day they email their class a question. The student must find the answer by using the Internet. Or, students can post the question for their peers. This is a fun way to learn, as well as master using the Internet and email. Published by *Judy Wood Publishing Company.*

The Tutor's Handbook: Math (Grade 2)
This helpful guide offers enrichment for students and includes: a sample tutoring session, creative tutoring strategies, reproducible work sheets and real-life math connections. Published by *Frank Schaffer Publications.*

First Steps in Missions, Vol. 6 with Tammie Worsham
Activities and ideas for Mission Friends and Teachers. This book offers fun and learning-based activities for home-schoolers, Vacation Bible Clubs, Christian schools and others. Published by Woman's Missionary Union

About the Author

Carolyn Tomlin has been writing and published since 1988. She has authored 14 books and over 3,600 magazine articles in magazines such as *Entrepreneur, Kansas City News, American Profile, Home Life, Mature Living, ParentLife*, and many others. She and Denise George are writing 14 books for the popular seminar, Boot Camp for Christian Writers. Her latest books are *What I Wish I'd Known Sooner: Parents, What I Wish I'd Known Sooner: Teachers* and *More Alike Than Different* (a story and coloring book for children.). Carolyn is married to Dr. Matt Tomlin, a Southern Baptist pastor. They have two adult children, Cindy Tomlin Coulston and Kevin Tomlin and six grandchildren.

You may contact Carolyn Tomlin at:
Carolyn's email address: Carolyn.tomlin@yahoo.com
Web Page: www.carolyntomlin.com
For writers: http://christianwritersbootcamp.blogspot.com
Beeson's website:
http://www.beesondivinity.com/bootcampforchristianwriters

Boot Camp for Christian Writers®

Boot Camp for Christian Writers® is a no-nonsense, basic, information-packed, series of all-day, one-day seminars that educate and equip Christian writers to write clearly, communicate effectively to a chosen audience, professionally approach magazine editors and book publishers with good ideas, and get articles and books published!

Founded in February, 2009, by Denise George and Carolyn Tomlin, Boot Camp for Christian Writers® is based on Colossians 3:12-17 and (Col. 3:23-24): "Whatever you do, work at it with all your heart, as working for the Lord, not for men... It is the Lord Christ you are serving."

George and Tomlin keep in close touch with their Boot Campers through email, and are available to answer questions, give advice, etc. Boot Campers can communicate with each other through the Boot Camp FaceBook Page. The Boot Camper Blogspot provides regular information on writing, tips, publishing trends, current writing news, photos, etc.

George and Tomlin teach using three modes of learning:

1. <u>Visual:</u> They offer the latest in technology with creative PowerPoint and KeyNote presentations;
2. <u>Auditory</u>: They present information in a comfortable classroom-style setting, and give question & answer opportunities after each seminar;
3. <u>Kinesthetic</u>: They provide printed handout materials to go along with their presentations, as well as personally-written books (like this one) that participants can purchase to gain deeper understanding, further information, and self-learning exercises to use at home.

Hundreds of people have already participated in these information-packed seminars! The seminars are exciting and fun, and writers enjoy meeting each other and comparing ideas! Our Boot Campers are writing confidently, contacting editors with magazine and book ideas, selling articles to magazines, and receiving book contracts from major publishers! They are also learning how to self-publish and promote their books to the world! Attend one of the Boot Camp for Christian Writers® seminars and become a lifetime member of the "Family of Christian Writers."

If you are interested in bringing together a group of writers in your area, and hosting a Boot Camp for Christian Writers® seminar, please email Denise George: cdwg@aol.com.

For more information, please see:

Beeson's Web site:
http://www.beesondivinity.com/bootcampforchristianwriters

Boot Camp FaceBook Page:
http://www.facebook.com/BootCampForChristianWriters

Boot Camp Blogspot: http://christianwritersbootcamp.blogspot.com/

Happy writing and may God bless you! Carolyn Tomlin

Your Seminar Notes: